For Tom
from
Marge Piercy
November 13,
1990

The earth shines secretly

Carolyn's Bouquet with Heliotrope, 1985

The earth shines secretly

A BOOK OF DAYS

Marge Piercy
Poetry

Nell Blaine
Paintings and Drawings

Z

ZOLAND BOOKS, INC.

Cambridge, Massachusetts

First edition published in 1990 by Zoland Books, Inc.
384 Huron Avenue, Cambridge, MA 02138

Poems by Marge Piercy are selected from the following collections published by Alfred A. Knopf, Inc.: *Living in the Open* ("Kneeling here, I feel good," "Beautiful weeper," "On Castle Hill"); *The Twelve-Spoked Wheel Flashing* ("Smalley Bar"); *The Moon is Always Female* ("The inside chance," "Rainy 4th," "September afternoon at four o'clock," "The perpetual migration," "The great horned owl"); *Stone, Paper, Knife* ("More that winter ends than spring begins," "Toad dreams," "In which she begs (like everybody else) that love may last," "The doe"); *My Mother's Body* ("Deer couchant," "Going into town in the storm"); and *Available Light* ("A low perspective," "The New Year of the Trees").

Special thanks are due the editors of the following journals, in which previously uncollected poems first appeared: *Images, Zone 3, The Poets Perspective, Yellow Silk, Calapooya Collage 12,* and *Country Journal.*

Library of Congress Catalog Card Number: 89-52050
ISBN 0-944072-10-0

FIRST EDITION
Printed in the United States of America

Cover: *Indian Summer, Gloucester* (1983) by Nell Blaine

Snow blink: that's light
hitting the bottomside of clouds,
when the earth shines secretly
like the moon, when white
fields glare at the sky.

Marge Piercy, "A low perspective"

Marge Piercy

Marge Piercy is the author of eleven books of poetry, including *The Moon is Always Female* and *Circles on the Water,* and nine novels, including her recent fiction *Gone to Soldiers* and *Summer People.* Translations of her books have been published throughout Europe. She has been a political activist for years—civil rights, anti-war groups—and is active in the women's movement. She travels regularly to give readings and workshops at colleges and festivals. Marge Piercy lives in Wellfleet, Massachusetts, with her husband, writer Ira Wood.

About her poetry: "I think Marge Piercy is one of the most important writers of our time, who has redefined the meaning of the female consciousness in literature and in so doing has begun to redefine the meaning of literature." – Erica Jong

About her fiction: "Here is somebody with the guts to go into the deepest core of herself, her time, her history, and risk more than anybody else has so far, just out of a love for the truth and a need to tell it." – Thomas Pynchon, writing on *Dance the Eagle to Sleep*

Nell Blaine

In the early 1940s, Nell Blaine left Richmond, Virginia (where she was born in 1922) to study with Hans Hofmann in New York. She showed early work at Peggy Guggenheim's Art of This Century and the Jane Street Galleries, quickly becoming an important figure in the abstract movement. In the 1950s her work was exhibited at The Tibor de Nagy Gallery with artists Helen Frankenthaler, Larry Rivers, Grace Hartigan, Fairfield Porter, Jane Freilicher, and Robert Goodnough and poets published by the gallery: John Ashbery, Barbara Guest, James Schuyler, and Frank O'Hara. After 1955 she showed at the Poindexter and Fischbach Galleries.

Nell Blaine's paintings have gradually become more figurative, and since the late 1950s she has worked most directly from nature. Her work can be viewed in the permanent collections of more than twenty museums, including The Metropolitan Museum of Art, The Museum of Modern Art, The National Museum of Women in the Arts, The Virginia Museum of Fine Arts, and The High Museum of Art in Atlanta.

In recent years she has divided her time between New York and Gloucester, Massachusetts.

Deer couchant

Seen from the air, when the small plane
veers in and hangs for a moment
suspended like a gull in the wind,
the dune grass breathes,
hue of rabbit fur.
The waves are regular,
overlapping like fish scales.
The Cape in winter viewed
from above is a doe
of the small island race
lying down but not asleep,
the small delicate head
slightly lifted. She rests
from the ravages of the summer
as a deer will take her ease after
the season of rifles and boots.

JANUARY

1

5

2

6

3

7

4

8

JANUARY

9

13

10

14

11

15

12

16

Snow, Yaddo, 1964

A low perspective

Snow blink: that's light
hitting the bottomside of clouds,
when the earth shines secretly
like the moon, when white
fields glare at the sky.

In winter the late light
reddens on the bay
from the small hidden sun.
The waters stain the puffball
clouds with rusty flames.

The angles surprise the eye.
The clouds look heavy,
smoky, lit from below.
A winter joy, beautiful
but ominous, like the flight

of the great horned owl
floating across the clearing

against the hunger moon,
like the cannonball reports of ice
freezing, thawing on the ponds,

the sharp encounter, the doe pawing
in the yard, fox in the path,
bluejay waking me by rapping
his beak on the glass, irate
diner summoning the slow waiter,

feed us now or we starve.
A light thatching of snow:
every grass blade prickles.
This low light hardens the black
in every twig to precision.

JANUARY

17

21

18

22

19

23

20

24

JANUARY

25

26

27

28

29

30

31

Studio in the Afternoon (Yaddo), 1964

FEBRUARY

1

2

3

4

5

6

7

8

FEBRUARY

9

13

10

14

11

15

12

16

Going into town in the storm

The sky is white and the earth is white
and the white wind is blowing in arabesques

through us. The world wizens in the cold
to a circle that stops beyond my mittens

outstretched on which the white froth
still dissolves. Up, north, left—

all are obliterated in the swirl.
The only color that exists clings to

your face, your coat, your scarf.
We ride the feathered back of a white goose

that flies miles high over the Himalayas.
Where yesterday houses stood of neighbors,

summer people, scandals still smouldering—

heaps of old tires that burn for days—

today all is whited out, a mistake
on a typed page. My blood fizzes in my cheeks

like a shaken soda waiting to explode.
Into any haven we reach we will carry

a dizziness, a blindness that will melt
slowly, a sense of how uneasily we inhabit

this earth, how a rise or drop of a few degrees,
a little more water or a trifle less, renders

us strange as brontosaurus in our homeland.
We are fitted for a short winter and then spring.

We stagger out of the belly of the snow
plucked of words naked and steaming.

FEBRUARY

17

21

18

22

19

23

20

24

FEBRUARY

25

26

27

28

29

The New Year of the Trees

It is the New Year of the Trees, but here
the ground is frozen under the crust of snow.
The trees snooze, their buds tight as nuts.
Rhododendron leaves roll up their stiff scrolls.

In the white and green north of the diaspora
I am stirred by a season that will not arrive
for six weeks, as wines on far continents prickle
to bubbles when their native vines bloom.

What blossoms here are birds jostling
at feeders, pecking sunflower seeds
and millet through the snow: tulip red
cardinal, daffodil finch, larkspur jay,

the pansybed of sparrows and juncos, all hungry.
They too are planters of trees, spreading seeds
of favorites along fences. On the earth closed
to us all as a book in a language we cannot

yet read, the seeds, the bulbs, the eggs
of the fervid green year await release.
Over them on February's cold table I spread
a feast. Wings rustle like summer leaves.

MARCH

1

5

2

6

3

7

4

8

The inside chance

Dance like a jackrabbit
in the dunegrass, dance
not for release, no
the ice holds hard but
for the promise. Yesterday
the chickadees sang *fever*,
fever, the mating song.
You can still cross ponds
leaving tracks in the snow
over the sleeping fish
but in the marsh the red
maples look red
again, their buds swelling.
Just one week ago a blizzard
roared for two days.
Ice weeps in the road.
Yet spring hides
in the snow. On the south
wall of the house
the first sharp crown
of crocus sticks out.
Spring lurks inside the hard
casing, and the bud
begins to crack. What seems
dead pares its hunger
sharp and stirs groaning.
If we have not stopped
wanting in the long dark,
we will grasp our desires
soon by the nape.
Inside the fallen brown
apple the seed is alive.
Freeze and thaw, freeze
and thaw, the sap leaps
in the maple under the bark
and although they have
pronounced us dead, we
rise again invisibly,
we rise and the sun sings
in us sweet and smoky
as the blood of the maple
that will open its leaves
like thousands of waving hands.

Frank and Anemones, III, 1974

MARCH

9

13

10

14

11

15

12

16

MARCH

17

18

19

20

21

22

23

24

More that winter ends than spring begins

Nothing stirs out of the earth,
yet the dogs are trotting in odd
pairs of schnauzer and spaniel;
in small packs with brisk intent
they cross the streets. All over
Cambridge you can hear them barking,
sniffing each other in greeting,
raising their muzzles to drink the air
and read the gossip columns of scent.

Pigeons too are strutting on roof
beams like animate sofa pillows
puffing and cooing as they court
in the storm gutter. The old cat
crouching wary on the stoop suddenly
turns on her back and squirming
white belly up rolls on the sun
heated concrete with a sensuous shudder.

MARCH

25

29

26

30

27

31

28

APARIL

1

2

3

4

5

6

7

8

Kneeling here, I feel good

Sand: crystalline children
of dead mountains.
Little quartz worlds
rubbed by the wind.

Compost: rich as memory,
sediment of our pleasures,
orange rinds and roses and beef bones,
coffee and cork and dead lettuce,
trimmings of hair and lawn.

I marry you, I marry you.
In your mingling under my grubby nails
I touch the seeds of what will be.

Revolution and germination
are mysteries of birth
without which
many
are born to starve.

I am kneeling and planting.
I am making fertile.
I am putting
some of myself
back in the soil.
Soon enough
sweet black mother of our food
you will have the rest.

APRIL

9

13

10

14

11

15

12

16

APARIL

17

21

18

22

19

23

20

24

Trees by Cottage, 1979

APRIL

25

26

27

28

29

30

Toad dreams

---

*That afternoon the dream of the toads rang through the elms by Little River
and affected the thoughts of men, though they were not conscious that
they heard it.* —Henry Thoreau

The dream of toads: we rarely
credit what we consider lesser
life with emotions big as ours,
but we are easily distracted,
abstracted. People sit nibbling
before television's flicker watching
ghosts chase balls and each other
while the skunk is out risking grisly
death to cross the highway to mate;
while the fox scales the wire fence
where it knows the shotgun lurks
to taste the sweet blood of a hen.
Birds are greedy little bombs
bursting to give voice to appetite.
I had a cat who died of love, starving
when my husband left her too.
Dogs trail their masters across continents. We are far too busy
to be starkly simple in passion.
We will never dream the intense
wet spring lust of the toads.

MAY

1

2

3

4

5

6

7

8

In which she begs (like everybody else) that love may last

The lilac blooms now in May,
our bed awash with its fragrance,
while beside the drive, buds
of peony and poppy swell
toward cracking, slivers of color
bulging like a flash of eye
from someone pretending to sleep.
Each in its garden slot, each
in its season, crocus gives way
to daffodil, through to fall
monkshood and chrysanthemum.
Only I am the wicked rose
that wants to bloom all year.
I am never replete with loving
you. Satisfaction
makes me greedy. I want
to blossom out with my joy of you
in March, in July, in October.
I want to drop my red red
petals on the hard black ice.

MAY

9

13

10

14

11

15

12

16

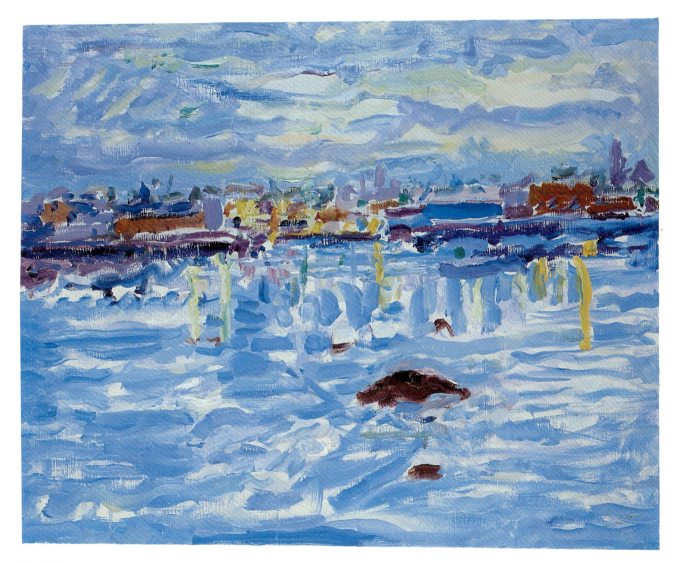

Blue Harbor, 1985

MAY

17

21

18

22

19

23

20

24

MAY

25

26

27

28

29

30

31

Softly during the night

Rain is tickling the leaves like the ghost of itself.
I wake to it and at first I think it is someone
muttering in my ear. It is a teasing caress
on the roof, a lover's hair brushing my belly,
a cat who raps your arm lightly with her tail
to call back your attention from the trivial book.

When I went to bed, the moon was bobbing, sinking
on long breaking waves of cloud. Salt hung
in the air, lightly stinging the eyes and nostrils.
Now it is dark in the fringed shawl of the rain.
I lie awake listening, for its liquid whisper
snags the attention more closely than clamor,

rain that slips in on the sly. The dawn sky
will be mauve, cloudless, clean as a new tent
just raised. Only the leaves on the roadside
bushes brushing my face with heavy drops of water
as I pass bear witness to what came and left
furtive as if it took instead of giving.

JUNE

1

5

2

6

3

7

4

8

Smalley Bar

Anchored a ways off Buoy Rocks the sailboat
bobs jaunty, light, little. We slide
over the side after scraping bottom.
The water up to our waists looks brown
ahead. We wade onto Smalley Bar.
I leave the men clamming and walk
the bar toward shore.

By the time I walk back straight out
from the coast of the wild island the tide
is rushing in. My shoes already float.
I walk the bar, invisible now,
water to my thighs. The day's
turned smoky. A storm is blowing
thick from the east. I stand
a quarter mile out in the bay with
the tide rising and only this
strange buried bridge of sandbar under me,
calling across the breaking grey waves,
unsure whether I can still wade

or must swim against the tide to the boat
dragging its anchor loose.

Unknown territory. Strange bottom.
I live on bridges that may or may
not be there under the breaking
water deepening. I never know
what I'll step on. I never know
whether I'll make it before dark,
before the storm catches me,
before the tide sweeps me out.
The neat white houses across the bay
are fading as the air thickens.
People in couples, in boxes, in clear
expectations of class and role
and income, I deserve no pity
shivering here as the water rushes past.
I find more than clams out on
the bar. It's not my sailboat
ever, but it's my choice.

JUNE

9

13

10

14

11

15

12

16

The wood thrush at twilight
calls from the nearest pine.
The air: birdsfoot violets
a languid white washed with blue.
You touch my nape
sliding your fingers
under my loose hair.
I am water
seeking the ground
where deep currents
swirl and eddy
under the sand.

JUNE

17

21

18

22

19

23

20

24

Dorset Garden with Blackbirds, 1964

JUNE

25

29

26

30

27

28

JULY

1

5

2

6

3

7

4

8

Rainy 4th

I am someone who boots myself from bed
when the alarm cracks my sleep. Spineless
as raw egg on the tilted slab of day
I ooze toward breakfast to be born.
I stagger to my desk on crutches of strong coffee.

How sensuous then are the mornings we do
not rise. This morning we curl embracing
while rain crawls over the roof like a thousand
scuttling fiddler crabs. Set off a
twenty-one tea kettle salute
for a rainy 4th with the parade and races
cancelled, our picnic chilling disconsolate
in five refrigerators. A sneaky hooray
for the uneven gallop of the drops,
for the steady splash of the drainpipe,
for the rushing of the leaves in green

whooshing wet bellows, for the teeming wind
that blows the house before it in full sail.

We are at sea together in the woods.
The air chill enough for the quilt, warm
and sweet as cocoa and coconut we make
love in the morning when there's never time.
Now time rains over us liquid and vast.
We talk facing, elastic parentheses.
We dawdle in green mazes of conversing
seeking no way out but only farther into
the undulating hedges, grey statues of nymphs,
satyrs and learned old women, broken busts,
past a fountain and tombstone
in the boxwood of our curious minds
that like the pole beans on the fence
expand perceptibly in the long rain.

JULY

9

13

10

14

11

15

12

16

Frog song

Waterlilies float like half moons
on Herring Pond silent as marble
where ragged and patchy alewives
drag themselves along in the spring
and finally home free, spawn.

We paddle our canoe swishing on flat
landing pads. The cups of the lilies
rise, dreams almost taking off
but held on their long balloon
strings anchored in fishy muck.

The canoe glides over dream lilies.
Oh havoc, oh crushing waste. But they
pop up behind us with drops of water
glittering. Translucent alewife
minnows quiver under them in hiding.

We slide over sky caught flashing
among pads. We loll on the outstretched
palm of summer. A dragonfly scouts us,
zips off while the sun leaves the gold
smear of its thumb on every sigh.

JULY

17

21

18

22

19

23

20

24

JULY

25

29

26

30

27

31

28

AUGUST

1

5

2

6

3

7

4

8

Platform Garden, 1988

AUGUST

9

13

10

14

11

15

12

16

On Castle Hill

As we wandered through the hill of graves,
men lost at sea, women in childbirth,
slabs on which were thriftily listed
nine children like drowned puppies,
all the Susan-B-wife-of-Joshua-Stones,
a woman in a long calico gown strolled toward us
bells jangling at waist, at wrists,
lank brown hair streaming.
We spoke to her but she smiled only
and drifted on into the overgrown woods.
Suppose, you said, she is a ghost.
You repeated a tale from Castaneda
about journeying toward one's childhood
never arriving but encountering

on the way many people, all dead,
journeying toward the land of heart's desire.

I would not walk a foot into my childhood,
I said, picking blackberries for you to taste,
large, moist and sweet as your eyes.
My land of desire is the marches
of the unborn. The dead
are powerless to grant us
wishes, their struggles
are the wave that carried us here.
Our wind blows on toward those hills
we will never see.

Hot, hotter

The world is a womb, hot and wet
and laboring to be delivered of August,
panting, gasping in the fever of afternoon,
sizzling night sweats and poached mornings.

Yet sweat only eases our bodies together,
oils us so we slide and skid bellies,
the bed a griddle where we hop, droplets
of ignited blood, minute's torches.

Waters flow over waters, currents melding.
Up from the rippled bottom an elbow juts,
a cockfish hunts the coral maze,
an anemone opens its fringed waving petals.

Heat asks for nakedness and nakedness
breeds inner heat releasing itself in friction.
So we make each other hotter and then cooler.
In the sticky knot of sheets we close in sleep.

AUGUST

17

21

18

22

19

23

20

24

AUGUST

25

26

27

28

29

30

31

Fox grapes

It is near the railroad bridge over the creek
where wild blue grapes run rampant up trees,
the ones the locals call fox grapes.
I have seen you pick them with your teeth.

You are poised in the old right of way,
your body a straight line out to the plume's tip
but for your jack of diamond's face, pointed,
wary, jutting at me sharp as a glass corner.

Our eyes meet. We stand each with our feet
loaded and ready to discharge into motion.
That look is opaque and piercing and curious.
We drink each other like whiskey, straight

and strong and blinding in the brain.
For a long time we hold each other stabbed
through as if by desire. Then you stir
and are gone in the baked grasses. All day

nothing human of words or touch pierces my brain
to that deep spot where your ember smoulders.
Your family is breaking. You start your wild
solitary fall when you hunt and run alone.

SEPTEMBER

1

5

2

6

3

7

4

8

September afternoon at four o'clock

Full in the hand, heavy
with ripeness, perfume spreading
its fan: moments now resemble
sweet russet pears glowing
on the bough, peaches warm
from the afternoon sun, amber
and juicy, flesh that can
make you drunk.

There is a turn in things
that makes the heart catch.
We are ripening, all the hard
green grasping, the stony will
swelling into sweetness, the acid
and sugar in balance, the sun
stored as energy that is pleasure
and pleasure that is energy.

Whatever happens, whatever,
we say, and hold hard and let
go and go on. In the perfect
moment the future coils,
a tree inside a pit. Take,
eat, we are each other's
perfection, the wine of our
mouths is sweet and heavy.
Soon enough comes the vinegar.
The fruit is ripe for the taking
and we take. There is
no other wisdom.

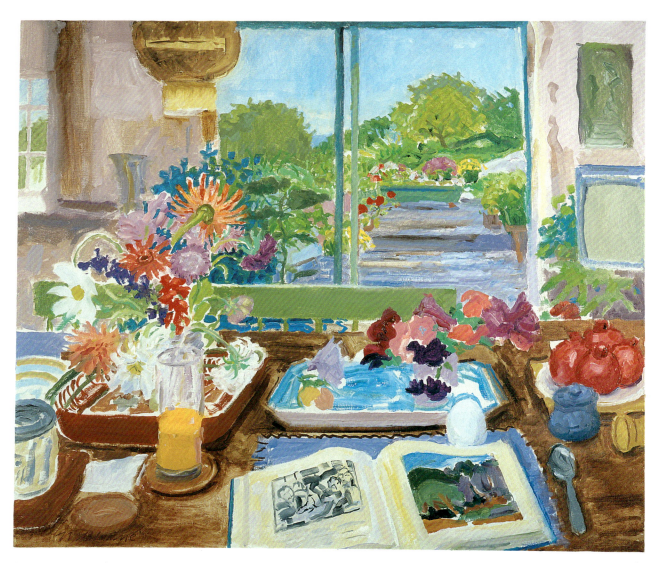

Summer Interior with Open Book, 1986

SEPTEMBER

9

10

11

12

13

14

15

16

SEPTEMBER

17

18

19

20

21

22

23

24

The perpetual migration

How do we know where we are going?
How do we know where we are headed
till we in fact or hope or hunch
arrive? You can only criticize,
the comfortable say, you don't know
what you want. Ah, but we do.

We have swung in the green verandas
of the jungle trees. We have squatted
on cloud-grey granite hillsides where
every leaf drips. We have crossed
badlands where the sun is sharp as flint.
We have paddled into the tall dark sea
in canoes. We always knew.

Peace, plenty, the gentle wallow
of intimacy, a bit of Saturday night
and not too much Monday morning,
a chance to choose, a chance to grow,
the power to say no and yes, pretties
and dignity, an occasional jolt of truth.

The human brain, wrinkled slug, knows
like a computer, like a violinist, like
a bloodhound, like a frog. We remember
backwards a little and sometimes forwards,
but mostly we think in the ebbing circles
a rock makes on the water.

The salmon hurtling upstream seeks
the taste of the waters of its birth
but the seabird on its four-thousand-mile
trek follows charts mapped on its genes.
The brightness, the angle, the sighting
of the stars shines in the brain luring
till inner constellation matches outer.

The stark black rocks, the island beaches
of waveworn pebbles where it will winter
look right to it. Months after it set
forth it says, home at last, and settles.
Even the pigeon beating its short whistling
wings knows the magnetic tug of arrival.

In my spine a tidal clock tilts and drips
and the moon pulls blood from my womb.
Driven as a migrating falcon, I can be blown
off course yet if I turn back it feels
wrong. Navigating by chart and chance
and passion I will know the shape
of the mountains of freedom, I will know.

SEPTEMBER

25

29

26

30

27

28

OCTOBER

1

2

3

4

5

6

7

8

OCTOBER

9

13

10

14

11

15

12

16

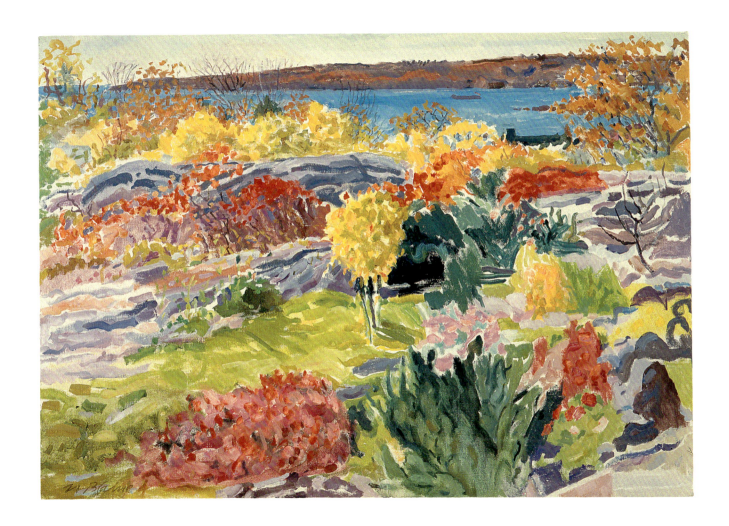

Indian Summer, Gloucester, 1983

OCTOBER

17

21

18

22

19

23

20

24

Beautiful weeper

Come under the willow
tree in the fall,
its yellow cataract
of languor: hair
of lady shuddering.
In the spring
the wands will brighten
early as forsythia.
Willow, willow by the water
your roots creep
into pipes and drains
to clog them
with your secret vigor.
Willow, willow shivering,
you look ethereal to survive,
you droop for a living
while underground your vast
root system thrives.
I want to be as little like you
as they will let me
except for your energy
striving for water to live,
willow,
sister willow.

Putting the gardens to sleep

We are putting the gardens to sleep,
harvesting the last hardy crops, the coles,
picking up the drip hoses, digging in lime,
manure, turning the soil over.

The jungles of productivity which whenever
we pass them nine months of the year
cackle like chickens to be fed our time,
pick me, weed me, thin me, mulch me,

now are quiet as rugs and have shrunk
to the size of a few hasty strides.
Without all the roughly improvised sculpture
of tomato towers, bean bowers and teepees

the eye passes over their furrows
and seeks the trees beyond. I still

have the feeling of playing hooky
every afternoon as I walk or read.

The soil relinquishes us in its sleep.
As a cat dreams of prey, it dreams
not of cabbages and peas but forest:
it longs to break into dock, lambsquarter,

work its way swiftly into grass, wild
rose, rum cherry, bristle with pitch pines,
thrust up at last its crown of climax oak.
Never tame, the soil is only captive.

OCTOBER

25

29

26

30

27

31

28

NOVEMBER

1

2

3

4

5

6

7

8

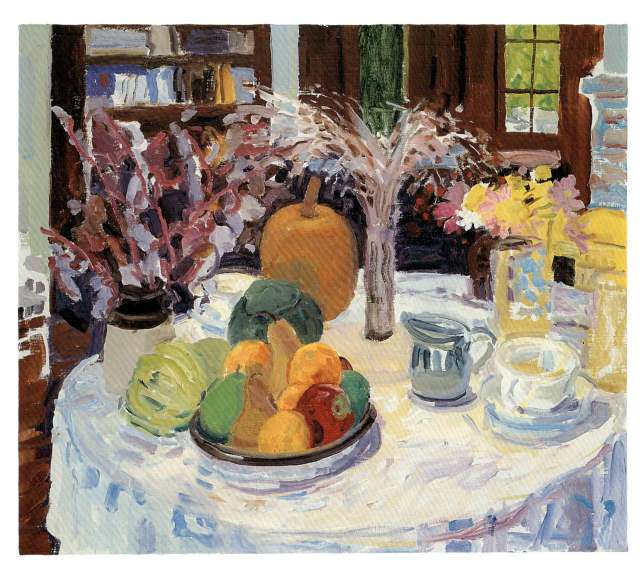

Autumn Table with Pumpkin, 1976

NOVEMBER

9

13

10

14

11

15

12

16

November Snow, 1987

NOVEMBER

17

18

19

20

21

22

23

24

The great horned owl

I wake after midnight and hear
you hunting: that sound seems to lodge
in the nape like a hollow bullet,
a rhythmic hooting plaintive as if
you seduced your prey by pity.

How you swoop from the dark of the trees
against the blackest blue sky of the November
full moon, your wings spread wide as my
arms, rough heavy sails rigged for a storm.
The moon blinds me as she glides in ripping
skeins of cloud. On your forehead you bear
her crescents, your eyes hypnotic
as her clock-face disc. Gale force winds
strip crispened leaves from the branches
and try the strength of the wood. The weakest
die now, giving back their bodies
for the white sheet of the snow to cover.

Now my cats are not let out after sunset
because you own the night. After two years
you return to my land. I fear and protect
you, come to harry the weak in the long dark.
Pellets of mouse and bird and shrew bone
I will find at the base of the pines.
You have come to claim your nest again
in the old white oak whose heart is thick
with age, and in the dead of the winter
when the snow has wept into ice and frozen
and been buried again in snow and crusted over,
you will give birth before the willow buds
swell and all night you will hunt for those
first babies of the year, downy owlets shivering.
Waking to hear you I touch the warm back
of my lover sleeping beside me on his stomach
like a child.

NOVEMBER

25

29

26

30

27

28

DECEMBER

1

5

2

6

3

7

4

8

The wind changes around

Yesterday the sky was larkspur velour.
The eye sank into it with languid ease.
The sun lay spooned like marmalade
　　on the drifts of leaves.
I found flowers of calendula, orange and green
eyed, the pointy blue of borage, last
brassy nasturtiums, although the first frost
is a month past, the maples plucked.
The broccoli thrust up new shoots.

This morning rain slithers over the windows.
The wind is spinning around toward the north
like a compass needle quivering.
I see them suddenly on the grape vine—

the snowbirds, the dark eyed juncos,
birds that fly down from the White
Mountains, the Maine firs and rock inlets
bringing the snow south.

They slip in, they join the confetti of finches,
of bluejays and nuthatches and chickadees
around the feeders. Jaunty and meek,
they are the jolly little omens
of hard times coming, warning
to fix the shed door and mulch the carrots
and kale, bring in more wood, for the snow
is coming like an army of occupation.

DECEMBER

9

13

10

14

11

15

12

16

DECEMBER

17

18

19

20

21

22

23

24

Clouds, Gloucester Harbor, 1974

The doe

On Bound Brook Island on December
24th, the air is mild and the sky
sags gently like a wet blanket
with promise of snow. Then
from a thicket of holly she bursts
leaping with her white tail
rising and dipping. Almost
the length of the valley to the bay
she runs before settling
in a copse. Poor cover here.
In summer she would only jump
the brook and sprint a few yards.
Thus the solstice blesses us
with her surviving the hunters
and the leap of our own hearts
that thud with her hooves as she bounds.

DECEMBER

25

29

26

30

27

31

28

List of plates

Frontispiece.
Carolyn's Bouquet with Heliotrope, 1985
20" x 19½" (51 x 50cm)
Watercolor
Mr. & Mrs. Theodore C. Rogers

1.
Snow, Yaddo, 1964
15" x 22" (38 x 55cm)
Ink and brush drawing
Mrs. Chauncy W. Durden, Jr.

2.
Studio in the Afternoon (Yaddo), 1964
35" x 45" (89 x 114cm)
Oil on canvas
Private Collection

3.
Frank and Anemones, III, 1974
16⅛" x 12¾" (41 x 32cm)
Ink stick and brush drawing
Private Collection

4.
Trees by Cottage, 1979
20" x 26" (51 x 64cm)
Ink and stick drawing
Private Collection

5.
Blue Harbor, 1985
16" x 20" (41 x 51cm)
Oil on canvas
Mr. & Mrs. Theodore C. Rogers

6.
Dorset Garden with Blackbirds, 1964
18" x 25" (21 x 64cm)
Ink and brush drawing
Maria S. Rost

7.
Platform Garden, 1988
18" x 24" (46 x 61cm)
Watercolor
Private Collection

8.
Summer Interior with Open Book, 1986
28" x 34" (71 x 86cm)
Oil on canvas
Mr. & Mrs. A.L. Aydelott

9.
Indian Summer, Gloucester, 1983
25" x 36" (64 x 91cm)
Oil on canvas
Mr. & Mrs. Theodore C. Rogers

10.
Clouds, Gloucester Harbor, 1974
15⅝" x 20⅜" (39 x 51cm)
Ink stick and wash drawing
Rosalind and Edwin Miller

11.
Autumn Table with Pumpkin, 1976
22" x 26" (56 x 66cm)
Oil on canvas
Jock MacRae

12.
November Snow, 1987
22" x 28" (56 x 71cm)
Oil on canvas
Mr. & Mrs. Theodore C. Rogers

Photographic Credits:
Rudolph Burckhardt (1)
Plakke-Jacobs (7)
Eeva/Inkeri (2, 11)
Lida Moser (6)
Otto Nelson (frontispiece, 4, 5, 8, 9, 12)
Nathan Rabin (3, 10)

1990

January
S	M	T	W	T	F	S
	1	2	3	4	5	6
7	8	9	10	11	12	13
14	15	16	17	18	19	20
21	22	23	24	25	26	27
28	29	30	31			

February
S	M	T	W	T	F	S
				1	2	3
4	5	6	7	8	9	10
11	12	13	14	15	16	17
18	19	20	21	22	23	24
25	26	27	28			

March
S	M	T	W	T	F	S
				1	2	3
4	5	6	7	8	9	10
11	12	13	14	15	16	17
18	19	20	21	22	23	24
25	26	27	28	29	30	31

April
S	M	T	W	T	F	S
1	2	3	4	5	6	7
8	9	10	11	12	13	14
15	16	17	18	19	20	21
22	23	24	25	26	27	28
29	30					

May
S	M	T	W	T	F	S
		1	2	3	4	5
6	7	8	9	10	11	12
13	14	15	16	17	18	19
20	21	22	23	24	25	26
27	28	29	30	31		

June
S	M	T	W	T	F	S
					1	2
3	4	5	6	7	8	9
10	11	12	13	14	15	16
17	18	19	20	21	22	23
24	25	26	27	28	29	30

July
S	M	T	W	T	F	S
1	2	3	4	5	6	7
8	9	10	11	12	13	14
15	16	17	18	19	20	21
22	23	24	25	26	27	28
29	30	31				

August
S	M	T	W	T	F	S
			1	2	3	4
5	6	7	8	9	10	11
12	13	14	15	16	17	18
19	20	21	22	23	24	25
26	27	28	29	30	31	

September
S	M	T	W	T	F	S
						1
2	3	4	5	6	7	8
9	10	11	12	13	14	15
16	17	18	19	20	21	22
23 30	24	25	26	27	28	29

October
S	M	T	W	T	F	S
	1	2	3	4	5	6
7	8	9	10	11	12	13
14	15	16	17	18	19	20
21	22	23	24	25	26	27
28	29	30	31			

November
S	M	T	W	T	F	S
				1	2	3
4	5	6	7	8	9	10
11	12	13	14	15	16	17
18	19	20	21	22	23	24
25	26	27	28	29	30	

December
S	M	T	W	T	F	S
						1
2	3	4	5	6	7	8
9	10	11	12	13	14	15
16	17	18	19	20	21	22
23 30	24 31	25	26	27	28	29

1991

January
S	M	T	W	T	F	S
		1	2	3	4	5
6	7	8	9	10	11	12
13	14	15	16	17	18	19
20	21	22	23	24	25	26
27	28	29	30	31		

February
S	M	T	W	T	F	S
					1	2
3	4	5	6	7	8	9
10	11	12	13	14	15	16
17	18	19	20	21	22	23
24	25	26	27	28		

March
S	M	T	W	T	F	S
					1	2
3	4	5	6	7	8	9
10	11	12	13	14	15	16
17	18	19	20	21	22	23
24 31	25	26	27	28	29	30

April
S	M	T	W	T	F	S
	1	2	3	4	5	6
7	8	9	10	11	12	13
14	15	16	17	18	19	20
21	22	23	24	25	26	27
28	29	30				

May
S	M	T	W	T	F	S
			1	2	3	4
5	6	7	8	9	10	11
12	13	14	15	16	17	18
19	20	21	22	23	24	25
26	27	28	29	30	31	

June
S	M	T	W	T	F	S
						1
2	3	4	5	6	7	8
9	10	11	12	13	14	15
16	17	18	19	20	21	22
23 30	24	25	26	27	28	29

July
S	M	T	W	T	F	S
	1	2	3	4	5	6
7	8	9	10	11	12	13
14	15	16	17	18	19	20
21	22	23	24	25	26	27
28	29	30	31			

August
S	M	T	W	T	F	S
				1	2	3
4	5	6	7	8	9	10
11	12	13	14	15	16	17
18	19	20	21	22	23	24
25	26	27	28	29	30	31

September
S	M	T	W	T	F	S
1	2	3	4	5	6	7
8	9	10	11	12	13	14
15	16	17	18	19	20	21
22	23	24	25	26	27	28
29	30					

October
S	M	T	W	T	F	S
		1	2	3	4	5
6	7	8	9	10	11	12
13	14	15	16	17	18	19
20	21	22	23	24	25	26
27	28	29	30	31		

November
S	M	T	W	T	F	S
					1	2
3	4	5	6	7	8	9
10	11	12	13	14	15	16
17	18	19	20	21	22	23
24	25	26	27	28	29	30

December
S	M	T	W	T	F	S
1	2	3	4	5	6	7
8	9	10	11	12	13	14
15	16	17	18	19	20	21
22	23	24	25	26	27	28
29	30	31				

1992

January
S	M	T	W	T	F	S
			1	2	3	4
5	6	7	8	9	10	11
12	13	14	15	16	17	18
19	20	21	22	23	24	25
26	27	28	29	30	31	

February
S	M	T	W	T	F	S
						1
2	3	4	5	6	7	8
9	10	11	12	13	14	15
16	17	18	19	20	21	22
23	24	25	26	27	28	29

March
S	M	T	W	T	F	S
1	2	3	4	5	6	7
8	9	10	11	12	13	14
15	16	17	18	19	20	21
22	23	24	25	26	27	28
29	30	31				

April
S	M	T	W	T	F	S
			1	2	3	4
5	6	7	8	9	10	11
12	13	14	15	16	17	18
19	20	21	22	23	24	25
26	27	28	29	30		

May
S	M	T	W	T	F	S
					1	2
3	4	5	6	7	8	9
10	11	12	13	14	15	16
17	18	19	20	21	22	23
24 31	25	26	27	28	29	30

June
S	M	T	W	T	F	S
	1	2	3	4	5	6
7	8	9	10	11	12	13
14	15	16	17	18	19	20
21	22	23	24	25	26	27
28	29	30				

July
S	M	T	W	T	F	S
			1	2	3	4
5	6	7	8	9	10	11
12	13	14	15	16	17	18
19	20	21	22	23	24	25
26	27	28	29	30	31	

August
S	M	T	W	T	F	S
						1
2	3	4	5	6	7	8
9	10	11	12	13	14	15
16	17	18	19	20	21	22
23 30	24 31	25	26	27	28	29

September
S	M	T	W	T	F	S
		1	2	3	4	5
6	7	8	9	10	11	12
13	14	15	16	17	18	19
20	21	22	23	24	25	26
27	28	29	30			

October
S	M	T	W	T	F	S
				1	2	3
4	5	6	7	8	9	10
11	12	13	14	15	16	17
18	19	20	21	22	23	24
25	26	27	28	29	30	31

November
S	M	T	W	T	F	S
1	2	3	4	5	6	7
8	9	10	11	12	13	14
15	16	17	18	19	20	21
22	23	24	25	26	27	28
29	30					

December
S	M	T	W	T	F	S
		1	2	3	4	5
6	7	8	9	10	11	12
13	14	15	16	17	18	19
20	21	22	23	24	25	26
27	28	29	30	31		

1993

January
S	M	T	W	T	F	S
					1	2
3	4	5	6	7	8	9
10	11	12	13	14	15	16
17	18	19	20	21	22	23
24 31	25	26	27	28	29	30

February
S	M	T	W	T	F	S
	1	2	3	4	5	6
7	8	9	10	11	12	13
14	15	16	17	18	19	20
21	22	23	24	25	26	27
28						

March
S	M	T	W	T	F	S
	1	2	3	4	5	6
7	8	9	10	11	12	13
14	15	16	17	18	19	20
21	22	23	24	25	26	27
28	29	30	31			

April
S	M	T	W	T	F	S
				1	2	3
4	5	6	7	8	9	10
11	12	13	14	15	16	17
18	19	20	21	22	23	24
25	26	27	28	29	30	

May
S	M	T	W	T	F	S
						1
2	3	4	5	6	7	8
9	10	11	12	13	14	15
16	17	18	19	20	21	22
23 30	24 31	25	26	27	28	29

June
S	M	T	W	T	F	S
		1	2	3	4	5
6	7	8	9	10	11	12
13	14	15	16	17	18	19
20	21	22	23	24	25	26
27	28	29	30			

July
S	M	T	W	T	F	S
				1	2	3
4	5	6	7	8	9	10
11	12	13	14	15	16	17
18	19	20	21	22	23	24
25	26	27	28	29	30	31

August
S	M	T	W	T	F	S
1	2	3	4	5	6	7
8	9	10	11	12	13	14
15	16	17	18	19	20	21
22	23	24	25	26	27	28
29	30	31				

September
S	M	T	W	T	F	S
			1	2	3	4
5	6	7	8	9	10	11
12	13	14	15	16	17	18
19	20	21	22	23	24	25
26	27	28	29	30		

October
S	M	T	W	T	F	S
					1	2
3	4	5	6	7	8	9
10	11	12	13	14	15	16
17	18	19	20	21	22	23
24 31	25	26	27	28	29	30

November
S	M	T	W	T	F	S
	1	2	3	4	5	6
7	8	9	10	11	12	13
14	15	16	17	18	19	20
21	22	23	24	25	26	27
28	29	30				

December
S	M	T	W	T	F	S
			1	2	3	4
5	6	7	8	9	10	11
12	13	14	15	16	17	18
19	20	21	22	23	24	25
26	27	28	29	30	31	

1994

January
S	M	T	W	T	F	S
						1
2	3	4	5	6	7	8
9	10	11	12	13	14	15
16	17	18	19	20	21	22
23 30	24 31	25	26	27	28	29

February
S	M	T	W	T	F	S
		1	2	3	4	5
6	7	8	9	10	11	12
13	14	15	16	17	18	19
20	21	22	23	24	25	26
27	28					

March
S	M	T	W	T	F	S
		1	2	3	4	5
6	7	8	9	10	11	12
13	14	15	16	17	18	19
20	21	22	23	24	25	26
27	28	29	30	31		

April
S	M	T	W	T	F	S
					1	2
3	4	5	6	7	8	9
10	11	12	13	14	15	16
17	18	19	20	21	22	23
24	25	26	27	28	29	30

May
S	M	T	W	T	F	S
1	2	3	4	5	6	7
8	9	10	11	12	13	14
15	16	17	18	19	20	21
22	23	24	25	26	27	28
29	30	31				

June
S	M	T	W	T	F	S
			1	2	3	4
5	6	7	8	9	10	11
12	13	14	15	16	17	18
19	20	21	22	23	24	25
26	27	28	29	30		

July
S	M	T	W	T	F	S
					1	2
3	4	5	6	7	8	9
10	11	12	13	14	15	16
17	18	19	20	21	22	23
24 31	25	26	27	28	29	30

August
S	M	T	W	T	F	S
	1	2	3	4	5	6
7	8	9	10	11	12	13
14	15	16	17	18	19	20
21	22	23	24	25	26	27
28	29	30	31			

September
S	M	T	W	T	F	S
				1	2	3
4	5	6	7	8	9	10
11	12	13	14	15	16	17
18	19	20	21	22	23	24
25	26	27	28	29	30	

October
S	M	T	W	T	F	S
						1
2	3	4	5	6	7	8
9	10	11	12	13	14	15
16	17	18	19	20	21	22
23 30	24 31	25	26	27	28	29

November
S	M	T	W	T	F	S
		1	2	3	4	5
6	7	8	9	10	11	12
13	14	15	16	17	18	19
20	21	22	23	24	25	26
27	28	29	30			

December
S	M	T	W	T	F	S
				1	2	3
4	5	6	7	8	9	10
11	12	13	14	15	16	17
18	19	20	21	22	23	24
25	26	27	28	29	30	31

1995

January
S	M	T	W	T	F	S
1	2	3	4	5	6	7
8	9	10	11	12	13	14
15	16	17	18	19	20	21
22	23	24	25	26	27	28
29	30	31				

February
S	M	T	W	T	F	S
			1	2	3	4
5	6	7	8	9	10	11
12	13	14	15	16	17	18
19	20	21	22	23	24	25
26	27	28				

March
S	M	T	W	T	F	S
			1	2	3	4
5	6	7	8	9	10	11
12	13	14	15	16	17	18
19	20	21	22	23	24	25
26	27	28	29	30	31	

April
S	M	T	W	T	F	S
						1
2	3	4	5	6	7	8
9	10	11	12	13	14	15
16	17	18	19	20	21	22
23 30	24	25	26	27	28	29

May
S	M	T	W	T	F	S
	1	2	3	4	5	6
7	8	9	10	11	12	13
14	15	16	17	18	19	20
21	22	23	24	25	26	27
28	29	30	31			

June
S	M	T	W	T	F	S
				1	2	3
4	5	6	7	8	9	10
11	12	13	14	15	16	17
18	19	20	21	22	23	24
25	26	27	28	29	30	

July
S	M	T	W	T	F	S
						1
2	3	4	5	6	7	8
9	10	11	12	13	14	15
16	17	18	19	20	21	22
23 30	24 31	25	26	27	28	29

August
S	M	T	W	T	F	S
		1	2	3	4	5
6	7	8	9	10	11	12
13	14	15	16	17	18	19
20	21	22	23	24	25	26
27	28	29	30	31		

September
S	M	T	W	T	F	S
					1	2
3	4	5	6	7	8	9
10	11	12	13	14	15	16
17	18	19	20	21	22	23
24	25	26	27	28	29	30

October
S	M	T	W	T	F	S
1	2	3	4	5	6	7
8	9	10	11	12	13	14
15	16	17	18	19	20	21
22	23	24	25	26	27	28
29	30	31				

November
S	M	T	W	T	F	S
			1	2	3	4
5	6	7	8	9	10	11
12	13	14	15	16	17	18
19	20	21	22	23	24	25
26	27	28	29	30		

December
S	M	T	W	T	F	S
					1	2
3	4	5	6	7	8	9
10	11	12	13	14	15	16
17	18	19	20	21	22	23
24 31	25	26	27	28	29	30

The earth shines secretly: A Book of Days is set in Bembo and Gill Sans, printed by Thomas Todd Company, Printers of Boston, Massachusetts on 80lb. Lustro and bound by Horowitz-Rae Book Manufacturers, Inc. of Fairfield, New Jersey. Book design by Susan Turner. Book production supervised by Nancy Robins.